THE HABITS OF
7
SEVEN
HIGHLY
ANNOYING
PEOPLE

by the editors of

BAD DOG PRESS™

Bad Dog Press
P.O. Box 130066
Roseville, MN 55113

e-mail: badogpress@aol.com & badogbook@aol.com

The Habits of Seven Highly Annoying People

First published in 1996

Printed in the United States of America.
96 97 98 99 00   5 4 3 2 1

Text: Tony Dierckins and Tim Nyberg
Illustrations: Tim Nyberg

ISBN 1-887317-02-3
Library of Congress Catalog Card Number: 95-83147

Warning: Contains humor, a highly volatile substance if
used improperly. Harmful if swallowed. All content is a
fictional product of the authors' imaginations. Any
resemblance between characters portrayed herein and actual
persons living, dead, or residing in New Jersey is purely
coincidental. Contents under pressure. Do not use near open
flame. Do not use as a flotation device, or at least avoid any
situations in which you would need to rely on a book as a
flotation device. Any typographic errors are purely
intentional and left for your amusement. Always say no to
drugs and, by all means, stay in school.

Contents

Preface

Annoying people. You know who we mean. They surround you. Your neighbors, your coworkers, even your friends and family—everyone you know has the potential to bug the heck out of you. And you probably do things from time to time that really bother those around you. Nobody's perfect. But what makes someone *highly* annoying?

Highly annoying people tend to bother almost everyone they know—and most people they've never met—to some degree. They're the coworkers everyone talks about at the water cooler. They're the relatives you'd rather not invite for the holidays. They wear bicycle shorts when they're not biking—and when it's apparent that biking could really help improve their health. Some repeat themselves over and over, driving their point home again and again until you just wish they'd stop, cease, finish, quit, get it over, and be done with it. Others repeat themselves over and over, driving their point home again and again until you just wish they'd stop, cease, finish, quit, get it over, and be done with it. They're the yippie little dogs of humanity, the tinfoil chewed by the filling-filled mouth of society, the human embodiment of fingernails down a chalkboard.

Don't hate the highly annoying. They can't help it. It's in their nature to annoy. Besides, they give you something to whine about with coworkers and family members. And who's to say you're not a little annoying at times yourself?

We recently sent teams of researchers across the nation to collect data about the highly annoying. Their work turned up some interesting—and frightening—habits practiced by the bothersome. Along the way they discovered seven of the most aggravating individuals one could care to meet. The following pages profile them for your benefit. Perhaps, by examining these seven people, we can all alter our behavior to become less of a nuisance to others. (We've changed their names to protect the less vexatious and avoid messy, annoying lawsuits.) But what can you do to help the highly annoying? First, identify the highly annoying people in your life: habitual practitioners of activities that greet your senses with all the pleasures of pouring lemon juice in a paper cut. Then buy them a copy of this book. Perhaps they'll get the hint.

—The Editors of Bad Dog Press

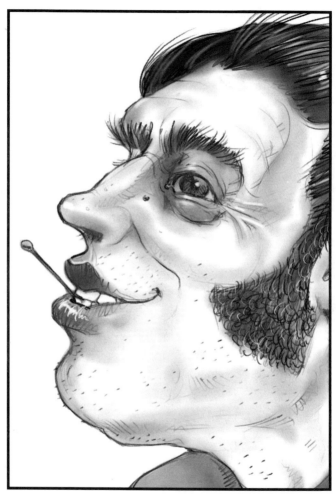

William "Wild Bill" Hodgkiss
Pavementum Porkumus Rex

William "Wild Bill" Hodgkiss
"King of the Road"

I was born to drive," says Wild Bill Hodgkiss from behind the wheel of his souped-up, candy apple red '74 El Camino. The Sedan, Michigan, native loves the road and he loves his car—from the pin-striping to the keystone mags to the "WLD BIL" vanity plate. And while he drives everywhere he goes—even across the street to visit the neighbors—not many people who know him enjoy sharing the road with Wild Bill.

You can't miss Bill on the road, especially if you're unfortunate enough to find yourself following him. Bumper stickers on either side of the vanity plate tell fellow travelers of Sedan's streets that Bill's other car is a Sherman tank, that the El Camino is protected from theft by Smith & Wesson, and that, profoundly enough, shit does indeed happen. Bill's front mud flaps display the silver silhouette of an apparently undressed and voluptuous young lady and those behind the rear wheels feature a gun-toting Yosemite Sam and the warning "Back Off!" Even without these visual hints, the blue smoke and dragging, coughing, spark-shooting muffler are dead giveaways that Wild Bill is steering the half car/half truck that just blew a stop sign and cut you off.

Yell as loud as you want: Bill can't hear you. He's added enough bass boosters, sub-woofers, and amplifier enhancers to his car stereo that it easily drowns out your complaints, disapproving horns, and the sirens of emergency vehicles. The driving bass of the El Camino's truck-sized speakers produces vibrations strong enough to force many dogs and small children to evacuate their bowels.

Sure, Bill's car is obviously bothersome. But what is it about Bill's specific driving habits that make him so highly annoying that he made the pages of this book? We've listed just a few to give you an idea of what it's like to share the road with a man who has his own unique interpretation of traffic laws and courtesies:

It doesn't matter when Bill pulls up to a four-way stop—it's his turn as soon as he has reduced his vehicle to a speed slow enough to resemble an attempt to stop.

Forces other drivers to make dangerous passing attempts by refusing to keep right with slower traffic.

Considers the employment of turn signals "optional."

Night or day, Bill likes to have the brights on, even if he's right behind another driver or oncoming traffic is within a hundred yards.

In backed-up highway traffic, Bill stays in the left lane to get ahead of other drivers and waits until he is twenty feet from his exit to merge right, forcing other drivers to stop for him, which subsequently causes traffic in both lanes to back up even further.

When negotiating a lane change, Bill begins his turn as he looks behind him to see if the road is clear.

Enjoys passing other cars, pulling in front of them, and then reducing his speed so he is actually going slower than those he just passed, thereby forcing them to tailgate him.

Rather than wait for traffic to clear, Bill enters roads by pulling out blindly in front of other cars, forcing them to suddenly reduce their speed, then once again proceeds to drive slower than the traffic behind him.

Once several cars are behind him, Bill slows the El Camino to five miles under the speed limit, especially in no-passing zones. He then steps on the brakes to indicate he does not appreciate being tailgated.

Talks on his car phone whenever possible, paying little attention to his driving and gesturing to make sure that other drivers notice he has, and is using, a car phone.

Wild Bill's annoying driving habits are by no means limited to the road. Rather than mess up the El Camino's ashtray, Wild Bill flips his cigarette butts out the car window. If, for whatever reason, the ashtray becomes filled with butts, he finds a quiet parking lot to dump them in. When he is without a passenger (which is most of the time, his wife reports), Bill tries his best to park the El Camino so its passenger door is no further than six inches away from the driver's side door of the vehicle on his right while remaining close enough to the car on his left to give his door protectors a hearty test. If he is in a hurry, able-bodied Bill has no problem parking in spots reserved for the handicapped. Once, Bill was apparently in so much of a hurry, he found no problem parking *on* the handicapped! (At his lawyer's advice, Bill refused to comment on this incident other than to say, "I honked!")

How did Bill pick up all these annoying habits?

"Taught him everything he knows" Clem Hodgkiss proudly claims. Clem, Wild Bill's father, is also proud of how he got his own license: "It was nineteen and twenty-seven, and boy, was it ever hot. On my fifteenth birthday I just took the trolley downtown to the courthouse, walked in, told 'em my name and address, and they give me the license. Twern't nothin' to it!" It would be five more years before Clem realized he needed glasses; and sixty-two accident-laden years later, he's still driving.

Bent with age at eighty-three, Clem has some trouble seeing over the steering wheel, lane changes have become a gamble, and he once left his right blinker on for more than seventy-eight miles—but that doesn't keep the old sparkplug from climbing behind the wheel of his Cadillac Eldorado whenever he needs to get somewhere, no matter how long it takes. "Sure, I drive a bit slow now," Clem says. "The way I sees it, I was here first and I'm going to take my time." Like his son, Clem enjoys the power of a good bumper sticker. His favorite? "I may be slow, but I'm ahead of you!" Long retired, Clem and his second wife Nora (Wild Bill's stepmother) spend their summers powering a giant Winnebago across the nation's two-lane highways, towing a boat and maintaining a steady ten miles an hour under the speed limit as traffic stacks up behind them.

So with the Hodgkiss family, it's easy to see that annoying driving habits (and a penchant for autos named with an "El" prefix) are genetically predetermined. And while that may not mean much to the average reader, the folks around Sedan aren't too happy about it. You see, Bill's twin daughters just turned fifteen and have their learner's permits, and Bill and Clem have promised to teach them to drive.

If you happen across Bill or Clem on the road, honk, wave hello, and try not to get too upset. If they're in a good mood they'll reply with their own blast of the horn, and you'll be treated to the irritating tones of either "La Cucaracha" or "Dixie."

Occupations Infested by Highly Annoying People

The list* on the facing page groups those occupations that do little to benefit society other than to provide the rest of us with an opportunity to ridicule those who hold such jobs. We don't mean to imply that all those working in these fields are annoying, but an overwhelming majority of them are at risk of becoming annoying if they stay with their chosen profession long enough.

* *Please note: order does not necessarily indicate a ranking.*

- Psychic Friend

- Used Car Salesperson

- Game Show Host

- Talk Show Host

- Talk Show Guest

- Infomercial Spokesperson

- "Drive Time" Radio Personality

- Insurance Salesperson

- Amway Dealer

- **Mime** (see also Performance Artist, Clown, Juggler, Magician/Illusionist, TV Weather Personality, and other assorted circus folk).

"Aunt" Edna Nusbaum

Sweetemus ad Nausium

"Aunt" Edna Nusbaum
Too Nice for Words

After "Aunt" Edna Nusbaum offered us pie and coffee for the fourth time, we knew our advanced field researchers had stumbled across a prime example of our "Dualistic Annoyance Theory": a person so darn nice she just plain bugs the heck out of you. Even after we insisted that we'd just had dinner and simply couldn't take another bite, she served us ice cream and apple pie with a crust so flaky it made Dionne Warwick's clairvoyant pals look like contributing members of society. But no matter how much we praised her pastry, Edna simply couldn't take a compliment.

"Too much cinnamon," she asserted, "I never

get that quite right." We just quietly ate our pie and ice cream, unable to bring ourselves to argue with Edna, a lady too nice for words.

"Can't stand the woman," complains Edgar Fitzsimmons. Edgar, Edna's neighbor in Shelbyville, Montana, for the past forty-seven years, complains that the hardest thing about living next to Edna is that she's always one up on you.

"It all started back in 'forty-eight, just after I moved in. I was laid up with fever and she stopped over with chicken soup. By the time the hallucinations stopped, it was the winter of 'forty-nine and she had quite a bit of snow built up on the walk. Well, I went over and shoveled her out to pay back her kindness. When I get through, she insists on paying me—won't take no for an answer—and she's got a whole pan of fresh-baked rhubarb crunch for me, and it ain't even rhubarb season! We've been goin' back and forth on this ever since," he finishes, patting a rather large stomach apparently caused by his neighbor's skills in the kitchen.

What other annoying niceties of Edna's drive her friends and family nuts?

Constantly hugs and pinches relatives, causing them to complain that she is overly affectionate.

Occasionally forces strangers to unwittingly agree with her relatives about her level of affection.

Edna never forgets a birthday or anniversary, making it necessary for everyone in her life to try to remember hers.

Always sends a card for every occasion (even though she usually has to make her "Groundhog Day" and "Arbor Day" cards by hand).

Responds to even the smallest gesture of

kindness by sending a "thank you" card.
Responds to "thank you" cards by sending one
of the "Thank You for the Lovely Thank You
Card" cards she's had printed up special.

Insists that you have yet another helping of her
tuna casserole long after you've eaten enough
of the flavorless, potato-chip-covered mush to
last you a lifetime.

Always uses adjectives like "wonderful" and
"absolutely marvelous" when describing mun-
dane, everyday occurrences: "I had the most
wonderful piece of toast this morning. You
simply must try this bread,
it's absolutely marvelous."

Always adds the imperative "You simply
must..." to the beginning of sentences
(see above).

To show what a "good" member of the church she is, Edna sings louder than anyone else, even the choir members.

Always sends the choir and clergy a basket of cookies, rendering the pastor and choir director unable to tell her that she sings too loud, off-pitch, and—often—the wrong verse.

The church officials' dilemma exemplifies the most annoying aspect of Aunt Edna, one that relates once again to our Dualistic Annoyance Theory: while she's nice to the point of being extremely vexatious, she's also so nice that you can hardly bring yourself to complain to her. Since no one has the nerve to tell Aunt Edna that her behavior is highly annoying, she continues to annoy. We all become her enablers.

Despite Edna's niceness, a person may feel justified complaining about one of her particularly annoying habits: her tendency to play the martyr. She precedes each gift-giving moment with the statement, "You can take it back," yet makes a big deal out of it when you do bring it back, explaining to others the trouble she went through to find the perfect gift and how no one appreciates her. Comfort level also brings out the martyr in Edna, as one of her favorite "nephews" and director of the Shelbyville Second Episcopalian Church choir, Jack Bachmeier, explains: "We try to take her out to dinner once or twice a year to thank her for all the cookies, but no matter where we go and what table we sit at, Edna's always asking 'Is it drafty in here, or is it me?' When we suggest moving to another table or switching places with someone else, she says 'Don't worry about me, I'll be fine.' Five minutes later she's saying, 'I should've brought a sweater,' and I'm about ready to take a handful of her peanut butter cookies—you know, the ones with the little fork prints in the top?—and shove 'em right down her yap!"

Sadly, or perhaps understandably, Edna never married, but she counts hundreds of souls among her extended family of "nieces" and "nephews." She insists that everyone call her "Aunt Edna," which brings up another sore spot for her neighbor. "I'm six years older than the woman and I'll be damned if I'll call her Aunt Anything!" Fitzsimmons yelled at us as we left his porch for our visit with Aunt Edna. "I'll call her Aunt Pain-in-the-Neck, though, that's what I'll call her!"

After our second piece of pie, Edna began to wear on us, and we began to fully understand the scope of our research—studying the highly annoying can really bug the heck out of a person.

After dessert, our new aunt asked us if there was anything she could get us to drink, and although we once again expressed our regrets, she began listing off possible beverage choices. She continued until we realized we'd get no more information out of her that night, and as we walked out the door and down the walk we could hear her liquid refreshment diatribe continue: "Or I could make some lemonade. You boys like lemonade? Of course, I'd have to stop by the grocer's first, and they're not really in season yet, are they? Lemons, I mean. How about a soda? I think I've got some Royal Crown cola here somewhere. You don't drink diet, do you? Because I don't drink diet, not with all the carcinogens in saccharin. Boy, that diet stuff will just kill ya. How about a Fresca? Doesn't that sound nice? A nice Fresca? Or maybe a ginger ale. That's always good. I remember when I was a little girl, my dad used to bring us ginger ale on Saturdays because it was a treat back then, it being the depression and all, and...."

As we got in the car we glanced next door to the Fitzsimmons' place, where Edgar sat on the porch wearing an "I told you so" smile and raising another forkful of rhubarb crunch to his mouth.

Annoying Relative Worksheet

Often, some of the most annoying people in our lives are relatives. Make a list below of some of your relatives and then list their annoying habits. Careful examination may find that annoying characteristics are actually genetic. This exercise may help you discover and then work on your own annoying tendencies.

Relative	Annoying Characteristic

Need more room? Feel free to photocopy this form.

A Note About Telemarketers

Careful readers will note that "Telemarketer," the most annoying occupation of all, doesn't appear on our list of "Ten Occupations Infested by Highly Annoying People." We omitted it from our list out of kindness: we didn't want those trapped in other highly annoying jobs to receive the same stigma associated with the phone salesperson. Poorly skilled and underpaid, these poor souls earn their living by placing unsolicited calls at inconvenient hours to innocent folks like you, trying to sell products you more than likely don't even want, let alone need. Furthermore, the term "telemarketing" was just made up so employers could make "phone sales" sound more attractive.

If you too find telemarketers highly annoying, and we know you do, you'll want to pick up a copy of Mrs. Millard America's *How to Get Rid of a Telemarketer*, coincidentally also published by Bad Dog Press.

(Please excuse the shameless, incredibly annoying act of using an entire spread to plug one of our other books.)

Joey "Little Tuna" Nunzio
Stupidimus Erectus

Joey "Little Tuna" Nunzio
Cluelessness Defined

When we knocked on his door for the Wednesday evening meeting we had set up a month earlier, our third highly annoying subject greeted us wearing a towel, his hair still wet with shampoo suds.

"Is it Thursday already?" he asked as he let us in. "Boy, the weekend just flew by, didn't it?"

When we offered to wait while he finished his shower, he looked at us inquisitively and said simply, "Shower?" So began our long, confusing night with Joey "Little Tuna" Nunzio of Lowland Heights, New Jersey, hands down the most annoyingly clueless person we encountered while conducting our study.

When we asked how he got his nickname, Joey offered little help. "I can't tell you that. It's not that I don't want too, you see, I just have no idea. Not even sure what it even means, really. Been drivin' me nuts for years. Might've had something to do with the time I got hung up in the fishing nets my dad used to hang up to dry in the back yard. Longest two weeks of my life, I tell ya."

Well, the longest two minutes of our research occurred during our introduction to Joey, as he didn't even attempt to restrain "Frothy," his obviously lonely and over friendly mastiff, from greeting us in his own special way.

"Look at that!" Joey exclaimed. "Ain't that cute? He likes ya, that's how come he plays that game with you. That's it, Frothy! Ride that leg! Ride it, boy!"

"Mom says Daddy's more special than most people," says Joey's sixteen-year-old daughter Angelica Rose Mary Margaret Nunzio, an extremely patient young lady Joey calls "Two-

Toes" for no apparent reason. Angie-Rose helped us out first by tying Frothy up in the backyard and then by acting as sort of an interpreter for her father. We asked her to explain just how "special" it is to live with her dad.

"The hardest thing to do with Dad is to go to the movies with him. He makes us sit right in the middle, but he gets up like a kajillion times to go to the bathroom or get popcorn or whatever, and everybody in the aisle has to move. Then he forgets where we're sitting and he, like, calls to Mom and me so he can find us. He constantly asks what the actors just said, and after you tell him, he asks you what they said while you were explaining what they said before. People are always going 'Sssssshhhhh' and throwing jujubes at us, and once this guy almost hit Dad when he refused to take off his hat. And even at home, if there's a movie on cable or something and Dad's seen it, he spends the whole movie telling you what is about to happen and saying the lines just before the actors say them. My uncles say I could probably move out if I had a job."

With Angie-Rose rambling on and her father staring blankly into the TV, we left the tape recorder running and came up with this list of Joey's most annoying habits:

Falls asleep watching TV, but if someone changes the channel, suddenly wakes and says, "I was watching that."

Leaves the TV on all day long with the volume quite loud even though he isn't even watching. Usually has the TV tuned to the station "Geraldo" is on.

Always hums the theme song to "The Patty Duke Show."

Spends the better part of the dinner hour recapping specific episodes of "The Patty Duke Show."

Stops in the middle of crowded sidewalks and hallways to chat, forcing everyone to move around him.

Insists on refrigerating even the smallest leftover portion of food no one wants to eat and keeps it in the refrigerator until it grows its own fur coat.

Tells extremely long jokes with punch lines that are hardly worth waiting for.

Tells extremely long jokes and forgets the punch lines.

When others tell a joke, he asks them to please tell it again or to at least explain the punch line.

His reply to the explanation of most punch lines? "I still don't get it."

At the supermarket, he manages to somehow always select several items that require price checks or forgets an item and runs back to get it, holding up the line in either case.

Leaves his shopping cart in the middle of one
aisle and wanders off to another one.

Forgets which cart is his and walks off with
one belonging to someone else.

Never returns his shopping cart to the cart corral.

Leaves shopping carts in the middle
of a parking spot.

Worst of all, Angie-Rose reports, are her father's
telephone habits. She's stood by, embarrassed, as
her father tied up the only pay phone and a line of
about a dozen phone-needy people formed
behind him. "He would occasionally glance at
those in the waiting line, give them this, like,
patronizing smile, and then turn back to the
phone and continue talking for like twenty more
minutes. I never thought ordering a pizza could
take so long."

Angie-Rose reports that her uncles constantly

complain to her about her father's ill-timed calls: "He's always recording new, silly messages on the answering machine, and then he calls his brothers and tells them to call back so they can hear the message. Or else he calls them while they're in the middle of watching their favorite show just to ask 'whatcha doing?' Once he called my aunt during the last ten minutes of 'Murder, She Wrote.' She didn't speak to him for three years." An early riser with nothing much to do, Joey is on the phone most Saturdays by 7 A.M., calling old friends just to say "hi." "Sure, once in a while people get mad at me," Joey says, "but you gotta keep in touch with friends. It's the wrong numbers that worry me. Boy, those people get mad. Makes you wonder what kind of a world we live in."

His phone habits have apparently affected his performance at the workplace, as Pete Dreisdale, Joey's boss at Pete's Pan Poached Pig Parts, explains: "After sales in his region dropped, we monitored his calls. He put people on hold to answer a call-waiting call, then forgot about them. He called clients, then immediately put them on hold. He promised to call customers right back, then didn't. And if he did remember to return the call, he forgot what he was going to tell them!" Joey now works in packaging.

Before we left we couldn't resist asking Angie-Rose about her father's nickname. After she stopped giggling, she told us that her uncles made her promise never to tell. When we waved good-bye to Little Tuna and Two-Toes, my partner made a little joke: "Say 'so long' to Frothy for us, and tell him I hope he gets a date soon!" As we walked down the path to the car, we could hear Joey Nunzio as he whispered to his daughter, "I don't get it."

Ultra-Annoying Moment in Modern Music

In the early 1990s, the pop star once called "Prince" (the former Prince Roger Nelson) changed his name to ♀, an unpronounceable graphic. Annoyed, the media refused to use his new symbol and began calling him "The Artist Formerly Known as Prince," thereby annoying readers, listeners, and television viewers throughout the world.

To make reading about ♀ less annoying (if that's possible without adding phrases like "vows to never make another movie written, directed by, and starring himself"), we suggest that everyone pronounce ♀ as "Tafkap" (taf•kahp), an acronym for **T**he **A**rtist **F**ormerly **K**nown **A**s **P**rince.

There. That's better. Thank you.

Evelyn Threadgood
Pickimus Uppimus

Evelyn Threadgood

The Neatnik

As we knocked at the door of our fourth highly annoying subject, the first thing we noticed was that the unmistakable scent of pine cleaner seemed to hang in the air like some kind of omen, warning us of the uncomfortable task ahead: spending several annoying hours within the stifling tidiness of the home of Evelyn Threadgood, neatnik extraordinaire.

"Sorry about the mess," Ms. Threadgood apologized as we entered her immaculate home. "I haven't had a chance to run the vacuum since this afternoon."

Besides the annoyingly clean pine-fresh smell,

even the most unperceptive visitor to Mrs. Threadgood's abode will notice how everything—and we mean everything—matches. She limits the species of tropical fish in the living room's tank so they match the sea foam green of the tank's rocks, which, by the way, match the accents in the drapes and upholstery. Even the covers of the magazines fanned out neatly on the coffee table had some hint of light green. And when we complimented her on her choice of Van Gogh's "Irises" above the couch?

"Is that what that's called? You know, it took me almost five months to find a horizontal print with that particular green in it. And, it gave me a chance to splash around a little blue. Van Gogh. Well, I'll be darned."

We had a tough time getting comfortable in Evelyn's living room, but not because she wasn't a perfectly nice host. Rather, it was the combination of August humidity and the plastic covers on the furniture that left us squirming through most of our get-together. Evelyn believes strongly in the protective value of plastic: plastic "walkways" cover high-traffic zones on all her carpets, plastic "corner guards" prevent walls and wallpaper from marring, and plastic "bumpers" keep doors from banging against anything except their jambs.

When she offered us tea, we peeled ourselves off the couch and followed her into the kitchen. "House rules: no eating in the living room," she explained. In Evelyn's kitchen, which features a color combination of cornstarch yellow and country blue, "cozies" are the rule. Evelyn sews her own matching covers for everything that has a home on the kitchen's counters and table: a cozy for the toaster, the coffee pot, the tape dispenser, the electric can opener, the microwave. Even the box with her cozy-making paraphernalia is housed within its own color-coordinated cloth cover.

"She'd cover the damn kids in cozies, if we had any," says her estranged husband, Al. "Or wrap 'em in plastic! With that woman it's 'a place for everything, and everything in its place'—or big trouble! She can't stand a mess, or at least what she thinks of as a mess. She spends her whole day straightening up. On weekends, I like to sleep in. Well, if I get up to use the bathroom, that woman has the bed made before I flush! I had to get out for a while just to stay sane."

Al has moved out of the house while he and Evelyn try to work out the differences in their definition of an acceptable level of clutter.

"Now I get up in the morning, close the bedroom door and, hey, who cares if the bed's made? No one sees it but me!" Al exclaims. "She used to practically follow me around the house, picking things up as I set them down. Worse, she starts picking things up before I'm done with them. She's recycled the paper before I get a chance to read it, and she's clearing the table before I've finished eating."

Besides keeping an overly neat house, what annoying habits of Evelyn's drove her husband to move out on his own? He helped us compile this short list:

Serves the same meals on specific days of the week—Sunday: roast beef, Monday: spaghetti, Tuesday: chicken, etc. (except Saturday: pot luck!).

Prewashes all dishes before putting them in the dishwasher.

Loads the dishwasher by placing dirty dishes in separate categories in order to expedite emptying it later—she even puts the silverware in their own separate baskets (one for spoons, one for forks, one for knives, etc.).

Constantly doing the laundry; in fact, if there aren't enough dirty clothes for a load, she goes through the house searching for things to wash.

Perpetually vacuuming.

Alphabetizes books, tapes, and CDs, etc., by author or artist and cross-references them by genre.

Organizes your stuff for you, whether you want her to or not.

Brings supermarket checkout lines to a
screeching halt as she leafs through her
coupon organizer for a chance at twenty cents
off each item the clerk attempts to scan.

Can't go to sleep if anything in the house is
out of order or if the bedroom's
closet door is open.

Susceptible to anxiety attacks if things
are out of place.

Everywhere you look: coasters!

Why haven't the Threadgoods had children, even
after nearly a decade of marriage? We asked Al if
perhaps his wife thought they'd be too messy.

"Never asked her, to tell you the truth. Fact is,
I think it has somethin' to do with makin' 'em in
the first place, what with the sheets gettin' all tan-
gled up and me havin' to get on her side of the
bed and all. As far as she's concerned, that whole
business is just too… Well, let's just say that with

Evelyn, there's a lot of tidying up to do after, so to save work we haven't had too many opportunities to get things started, if you know what I mean."

We thought it was unfair to let Al have the last word on their childless condition, but just as we were about to ask Evelyn for her side of the story, my partner accidentally missed the coaster as he set down his tea. Before we noticed that fateful mistake, Evelyn had slipped into a full-blown anxiety attack. We quickly set the cup in the coaster and wiped up the tiny ring of tea on the counter, but Mrs. Threadgood continued to convulse.

Fortunately, she'd been through this many times before and knew just what to do. She slipped a hand into her plaid housecoat (which matched her slippers perfectly, by the way) and pulled out a small paper sack. After breathing into the bag for a few minutes, she regained her composure, apologized, then neatly folded the paper bag and returned it to its proper place.

After that, we found an excuse to leave and waved good-bye to the most annoyingly neat person we know. As we pulled away I happened to glance in the rearview mirror, where I caught a final glimpse of Mrs. Threadgood as she swept up the street where we had parked.

Right: While neatniks will find the page on the right particularly pleasing, persnickety book lovers will find it absolutely annoying. While The Chicago Manual of Style, *the "Bible" of the publishing industry, specifically allows for blank left pages, blank right-hand pages are a big "no no."*

It's okay for this page to be blank.

Ten Highly Annoying
Historic Figures

From party-crashing Greeks arriving in big wooden horses to Ross Perot's 1992 election bid, history books teem with accounts of the extremely bothersome. The following brief biographies represent our choices of the ten most highly annoying persons of all time:

Thespis *(c. sixth century B.C.)*

Considered the greatest actor of ancient Greece (hence the term "Thespian"), Thespis helped establish the popularity of Greek tragedy, which inspired the development of Western drama. Consequently, however, this also aided the development of mime.

Alexander the Great *(356-323 B.C.)*

As king of the Macedonians, Alex wreaked havoc on the Middle East before it was considered "middle," let alone "east." He makes the list because we figure anyone who called himself "great" had to be pretty annoying to be around.

Caligula *(A.D. 12-41)*

Roman Emperor from a.d. 37 to 41, Caligula made an annoying name for himself ("Caligula") by taking his senators' homes and wives and having an affair with his sister. He was also in love with his horse. Besides bothering other Romans, he made our list because we couldn't pass up an opportunity to mention a guy who was in love with a horse.

Leif Eriksson *(c. A.D. 1000)*

A leader among Vikings (fierce Norseman who bothered Europeans by plundering villages all along the European coast for almost 200 years), Eriksson "discovered" North America long before Columbus, subsequently introducing the Norse culture—and therefore, lutefisk—to the new world.

William the Conqueror
(A.D. 1028-1087)

By leading the Norman Invasion of 1066, Bill introduced French as the official language of the court of England, therefore infusing the English language with annoying French terms like *annoy* (from the Middle French *enuier*, "to make loathsome").

Genghis Khan *(A.D. 1162[?]*-1227)*

With his Mongol army, Khan conquered Asia and much of Europe, disrupting picnics wherever he rode. Also known as "The Great Khan" (see "Alexander," above).

*Editor's Note: Our editorial consultant points out that Khan continues to annoy researchers, as historians list his birth year as A.D. 1155, 1162, and 1167. Apparently Genghis annoyed his mother with a particularly difficult delivery.

John Lackland *(A.D. 1167-1216)*

King of England from 1199 to 1216, John submitted to political pressures and signed the Magna Carta in 1215, limiting the rights of British kings. This action eventually led to providing the royal family with far too much free time. Less than 800 years later, tabloid accounts of their extramarital exploits annoy the entire English-speaking world.

The French.

Richard Burbage *(A.D. 1567-1619)*

As a principal actor and partner in William Shakespeare's Lord Chamberlain's Men theater-company, Burbage consequently helped popularize the idea that actors of all shapes and sizes should wear tights.

Napoleon Bonaparte *(A.D. 1769-1821)*

The French emperor best known for losing at Waterloo and apparently having an itchy stomach rash, Napoleon and his armies terrorized much of Europe, thereby infusing Europe with annoying Frenchmen.

Adolf Hitler *(A.D. 1889-1945)*

Although he conquered France in 1939, Hitler annoyingly established the Vichy government (essentially a puppet of Germany) to govern defeated France, thus providing Claude Raines, a Frenchman, with a substantial role in the otherwise flawless *Casablanca*.

Maximillion Von Pipecrooner

Nonrespectus cum Populum

Maximillion Von Pipecrooner
Mr. Aggressive

It's not just that he's a loudmouth know-it-all," complains Babs Woodcock, former secretary of Maximillion Pipecrooner, our study's "Mr. Aggressive." "He's a loudmouth know-it-all who argues his point even after he's been proven utterly wrong!"

What does Mr. Pipecrooner say about his ex-assistant's accusations? "The woman's obviously nuts. I mean, that's why she can't keep a job, you know. Not once in six months did she ever make my coffee with the right ratio of cream to sugar. Never!"

When we met with Max, it was the middle of a typically busy workday for him, and as we followed him through the office, he gave orders, canceled appointments, rescheduled meetings, rejected proposals, postponed projects, criticized campaigns, and generally left a path of stress and tension in his wake. He would occasionally stop suddenly and in mid-sentence, pull out the tiny tape recorder he keeps in his breast pocket, and make another "note," such as: "Idea: hold power lunch to set up conflict between Research and Marketing; clearly imply winner gets larger budget. Question: what tie to wear?"

On the phone, Max insists on using the "speaker" feature, seemingly so he can concentrate on activities other than listening to whomever he's speaking to. And although we cataloged these along with dozens of potentially annoying habits in his behavior, current subordinates in Max's department had nothing but good things to say about their boss.

"Well, they're scared, obviously," Babs contends. "He's in control and he'll go to any ends to make sure they know that."

How's that, Babs?

"Mostly with contradictory behavior and subliminal attacks at others' self-esteem."

For example, Babs?

"Well, meetings are the worst," she claims. "They start when he's ready, usually about twenty minutes after they were scheduled. First off he says he has to leave early, cuts the agenda, and complains about things that haven't gotten done since the last meeting—things he took off the agenda last time. When it's time for other people to talk, he times them—actually pulls out a stopwatch and clocks them, never looking at the person speaking. When there's a call for a decision, he asks for more information, forms subcommittees, and tables the issue for the next meeting. Usually the most that gets done at meetings is the scheduling of more meetings. When it's over, he complains that meetings never start on time and says he should hire new people who can stick to agendas."

And if a meeting ever does get down to brass tacks? Well, let's let Babs vent some more anger, shall we?

"Well," Babs starts after a deep breath, "if someone does come up with a good idea, he spends ten minutes explaining why it won't work and what's wrong with the person who came up with it. Then he announces a plan that's almost exactly the same, only he words it a little differently and spends another ten minutes explaining why his is the better idea. If a project succeeds, he takes full credit, if not for the idea itself, then for his guidance. If it fails, he finds someone to blame, even if it was entirely his idea."

But how about Max's behavior outside the office? Is he just as annoyingly aggressive? We spent a Saturday afternoon with Max and came up with this list:

Begins most sentences with "Be a doll, won't you, and get me…"

Never seems to have a positive word to say about anything or anyone but himself.

Frequently asks, "You know what your problem is, don't you?" then proceeds to explain.

Constantly says, "You know what I'm talking about, don't you?" yet obviously doesn't really care whether you know what he's talking about.

Laughs out loud while reading; then, when you inquire as to the source of the humor, he replies, "Oh, nothing."

Makes others stop and read everything he thinks is so darned funny—no matter what they may be doing at the time.

"Pump" handshakes for an uncomfortably long time while moving his face within six inches of yours.

Reads over your shoulder.

Breathes hot coffee and cigar breath down your neck while reading over your shoulder.

At the supermarket, he races to get his overly filled cart to the checkout line in front of others, even if they have only a few items.

Finishes sentences for others.

Finishes your sentences for you— incorrectly.

Closes threatening letters with "Warmest regards...."

Always threatens to sue people over the smallest issue whenever he feels he has been "wronged."

Actually sues people.

But is it simply fear that keeps his current underlings silent? Could it be that simple?

"He's playing them," Babs says. "Likes to be 'one up' on everyone—make sure everyone else always 'owes' him something. Like, he'll do something for you 'out of the kindness of his heart,' but then he expects favors and preferential treatment in return. It's just another way to control people."

Sounds like Babs is more than a little disgruntled, doesn't it?

"Don't feel sorry for me," she says. "I love my new job, and they treat me so much better here. The stress in my life has been more than cut in half, and I'm starting to feel good about myself. The more I think about it, the more I feel sorry for Max."

After spending almost two days with Mr. Pipecrooner and then watching Babs merrily perform her new duties at the post office, we couldn't agree more.

An Apology (sort of)

Careful readers may have noticed that we did not include any women on our list of "Ten Highly Annoying Historic Figures." We apologize if this omission has offended anyone. Certainly history has seen its share of annoying women. One need only mention Lizzie Borden, Sally Struthers, and J. Edgar Hoover to make that point.

However, the issue arises that since men have historically written the history books, depictions of historic women in said history books may be unfair or even nonhistoric. Certainly some of Mary Todd Lincoln's episodes (or "more coal for the crazy train" as Abe was often heard to remark) have been exaggerated over the years. To be fair, we did not include women (except French ones) in order to avoid perpetuating such misinformation, thinking that some readers would in fact be pleased by our list's high number of white European males.

Some purveyors of so-called "political correctness," however, would have us go even further, to the point of objecting to the term "history" itself, preferring the newly coined "herstory." This, of course, has its roots in the annoying misinterpretation that "history" is the pasting together of "his" and "story."

Actually, "history" comes from the Latin *historia*, which comes from the ancient Greek *histor* or *istor* meaning "knowing, learned." The French, annoyingly, have their own version, *histoire,* meaning "a narrative of past events." Ironically, the gender-based languages (which annoyingly classify nouns as feminine, masculine, or [ouch!] neuter) from which "history" derives consider the word feminine in form. Furthermore, it is "story" that is derived from "history," in the same way "squire" came from Englishmen too annoyingly busy driving on the wrong side of the road to pronounce the first syllable of "esquire."

Unfortunately, no matter what annoying role thousands of years of patriarchy has played in the development, or lack thereof, of public rest room line management, gender equality cannot be achieved through linguistic acrobatics. And so we find words like "herstory" annoyingly overzealous.

We apologize if this apology offends anyone involved in the womyn's movement.

It may also annoy picky readers to know that we actually listed eleven anoying historic figures. If the French weren't so darn annoying we'd've had an even ten.

Vicki "Moon Child" Howenstein

Politicus Correctimus ex Tedium

Vicki "Moon Child" Howenstein
The Earthy Artist

W hen we met with Vicki Howenstein at Bucky's House of Beef in her adopted home town of Lao-tzu, New Mexico, she insisted that we call her "Moon Child." She also insisted that we go somewhere else to dine, as Vicki, a strict "vegan," had philosophical differences with the predominately red-meat menu at Bucky's. Forty-five minutes later, after scrutinizing the menus of several other restaurants for political improprieties, we pushed aside some of her cats and sat down to organic salads in Moon Child's apartment, conveniently located just down the street from the Whole Good Earth Co-op where we bought the produce. Vicki washed down her roughage with sips from her ever-present bottle of mineral water, which she drinks from throughout the day in order to cleanse herself from any "poisons" she may accidentally ingest.

"I believe in that old adage 'the body's a temple,'" explains our study's quintessential earthy artist, "and taking care of mine is just one way I worship The Goddess."

Vicki may consider herself a home to a neo-feminist deity, but we think of her as an annoying collection of inconsistencies. Although her parents both come from European stock, she adorns herself in the ceremonial garb of various Native American cultures. Before settling on "The Goddess," Moon Child spent much of her adult life exploring various religious options—she has practiced Judaism, Buddhism, Episcopalianism, Taoism, Sikhism, Snake Handling, and, until it taught her the true meaning of "sacrifice," the ways of the Aztecs.

Perhaps Vicki's "eclectic" taste in religions stems from her meandering educational background. She changed her major seven times before graduating with a B.F.A. in theater with a focus on both mime and the *commedia dell'arte*. During her nine years in and out of college and psychotherapy, she also studied eighteenth-century French poetry, philosophy, Sanskrit, abnormal psychology, women's studies, and Cherokee before "finding herself" as an actor.

"There's nothing more real to me than creating a role, nothing so self-satisfying as losing myself to bring a fictional character to life. I feel that I'm really being true to myself—really being me—when I'm up there being someone else. Wait, I mean… Oh, wow. That was profound, don't you think? Don't you think that was profound, what I said, I mean, about being myself when I'm someone else, you know?… Wow."

Actually, we found Moon Child's comments more telling than profound. Some of Vicki's former classmates found her habits profoundly annoying, and we found them more than willing to share some of her more bothersome traits.

"She's always 'on,' you know?" complains an

ex–study partner who asked that we not use her name (mostly because she hasn't decided on one yet; she too was cataloged as part of our study for her use of "uptalk"—the tendency to make every sentence sound like a question—and her insertion of "like" whenever she feels the need). "Like, everything she says or does is a chance to perform? And she's always telling you about your aura and, like, that there's this deeper meaning to everything you say? Like, you say something, and then she goes 'That's deep' and then she starts telling you all this stuff you really meant even though you only meant just exactly what you said and maybe not even that much, you know?"

Vicki's unnamed and ever-questioning study pal and other former classmates helped us compile this collection of Moon Child's more vexatious activities:

Refers to celebrities she has never met by their first names or nicknames (for example, she calls Francis Ford Coppola "Franky").

Names her cats using domestic titles ("Mr. Boots" and "Ms. Whiskers," for example)

When making a point, adds the interrogative "don't you think?" to the end of sentences, forcing others to comment on her statement.

Delays bathing and wears the same clothes for several consecutive days to "save water."

Insists that wearing underarm deodorant is "unnatural."

Berates those who smoke cigarettes, yet smokes clove cigarettes at parties, waving the foul-smelling butts about as if they were some kind of prop.

Sings along with every song on the radio, even those well outside her vocal range.

Sings along with every song on the radio, even if she doesn't know the words.

Makes up her own lyrics whenever she doesn't know the words to songs.

Peppers her sentences with famous lines from plays appeared in.

When ordering in ethnic restaurants, she overly pronounces menu items with "correct" accents.

Returns from European vacations speaking with a foreign accent.

Returns from domestic vacations speaking with a foreign accent.

Returns from the supermarket speaking with a French accent.

Yes, even the way Vicki speaks, her past classmates claim, can annoy the heck out of you. We found ourselves forced to agree. The indeterminable "accent" of Moon Child's speech renders confusion among those she meets, as it drifts from Southern Belle to British Sophisticate to New England Socialite depending on the topic of conversation. Her siblings (who, like Vicki, were born and raised in Flushing, New York) assure us that Vicki is not a Paris-born "Army brat" nor is French her native language as she claims.

And when Vicki's not being pretentious? Her ex-classmate says Moon Child spends her time putting people down and fishing for compliments. "She's always cutting down everyone she meets, you know? And then she cuts herself down so other people will say nice things about her, right? And then she wonders, like, why she can't get a date, you know?"

A psychologist we consulted for an explanation of Moon Child's behavior contends that Ms. Howenstein may suffer from a combination of overdeveloped ego and low self-esteem. We asked Vicki herself why she has so many weekends and evenings free to bond with her cats.

"It's these pants. They make me look fat, don't you think? I look fat, don't I?"

We spent the rest of our visit reassuring Vicki that her appearance had nothing to do with her inability to get a date (or an acting job, for that matter). As we left, she expressed her gratitude for our encouraging words: "Thank you, boys. I've always relied on the kindness of strangers." We took off before you could yell "Stella!"

Public Service Announcement

We'd like to take this space to recognize perhaps one of the most annoying people in all of the performing arts, a man synonymous with "mime": France's own Marcel Marceau.

Enough with the box, Marcel. There's no wind. You're not pulling any rope. We're not buying it.

Big Bob Cornfedder

Homo Repulsimus

Big Bob Cornfedder
The Inconsiderate Slob

There's just no living with him," says Marilyn "Debbie" Newbauer-Cornfedder-Phelps, the former wife of Big Bob Cornfedder, our final highly annoying subject. She should know: married to Bob for almost twelve years, Debbie witnessed firsthand some of the most annoying habits we've encountered in our research, behavior that forced us to label Bob an "Inconsiderate Slob."

We've saved the best—or worst—for last. Big Bob, a long-time resident of Conduit, Wyoming, has more annoying traits than any of the other highly annoying people we had the misfortune to meet during our long months of research.

Our visit with Big Bob was brief, our stomachs upset. As we asked questions, Bob not only took the opportunity to work on his clogged pores, but also offered unnecessary commentary as to his success. He also took the time, and several different fingers, to clear his nasal passages as we talked, all the while wiping his harvest on the furniture. Soon we were out the door with a clear idea why Debbie chose to end their marriage and not just a little touch of nausea.

"It's more than a question of hygiene," Debbie says. "You really can't go through life complaining about the little things. It's just that with Bob, there's so many little things that marriage with him was one big ugly, annoying thing. For example, I don't really mind that he bites his fingernails. I can ignore that. But when he started chewing mine, I decided enough was enough."

For Debbie, life with Bob was one long test of patience, especially in the bathroom.

"He squeezes the toothpaste tube in the middle. He leaves the cap off. He leaves two sheets of toilet paper on the roll or gets a new roll but does-n't put it on the dispenser. If he does, it's going the wrong way. He never flushes. Sometimes I even had to use a plunger to help the toilet do its job. Still, if that had been the worst of his habits, I'd still be with the big guy. But his, how shall I say this, 'bathroom aim' left much to be desired, and I appreciate a dry seat. I hear all these women at work complain that their husbands never put the toilet seat back down—well, I'd've gladly put up with a little seat inconvenience if he would've lift-ed that seat up once in a while."

When we met with Debbie, now remarried and decidedly happier, she was preparing for her upcoming appearance on a future installment of the "Ricki Lake Show," tentatively titled "I Left My Husband Because He's an Annoying, In-considerate Slob and I Simply Couldn't Take It Any More!" We combined Debbie's inventory of laments with our research of his neighbors' and coworkers' complaints to develop this abbreviated list of Big Bob's more aggravating activities:

Leaves his dirty clothes strewn across the bedroom and bathroom, then complains when he has no clean clothes to wear.

Never relinquishes his control of the remote control.

Makes nasal, "snorting" noises when he laughs. If he's not snorting when he laughs, it's probably because he's blowing root beer through his nose.

Never leaves the couch, but constantly begins sentences with "As long as you're up...."

Outdoors, Bob clears his nose by closing one nostril with his finger and blowing hard.

Indoors, Bob uses his sleeve as a handkerchief.

Since he can't smoke cigars in the office, Bob chews tobacco, using pop cans as spittoons.

Pours himself the last of the office coffee but doesn't make another pot.

Leaves the empty coffee pot to scorch on the burner.

Borrows tools and fails to return them.

Borrows tools and returns them in a state of disrepair.

Borrows tools and then lends them to someone else.

Coughs and sneezes in crowded elevators, then asks a friend to "remind me to get some antibiotics."

Those who have suffered through a dining experience with Big Bob have been treated to a virtual symphony of annoying traits. He sniffs. He snorts. He slurps. Sometimes he sniffs and snorts after slurping. For some reason restaurants remind him of past surgical procedures, which he then describes to his dinner companions. Often, his descriptions are loud enough to be heard in detail three tables away. He asks to sample others' food, then later applies medication on his frequent "cold sores."

Once the meal's over, the dining experience doesn't get any better. Bob enjoys a cigar after he eats, but his budget doesn't allow for particularly aromatic smokes, nor does he wait for his companions to finish eating before he lights up. When he notices a discouraging look, he says, "You don't mind if I smoke, do you?"

When the bill arrives, Bob insists on buying, then "discovers" he has left his wallet at the office. On the way out of the restaurant, Bob always forces a loud belch, which he follows with the same tired old joke: "Now that's the sign of fine dining: just as good coming up as it was going down—almost better the second time around!"

At parties, Bob "double dips" chips and veggies, and Debbie complains that he "backwashes" into shared drinks. Since their divorce, Bob's been eating alone for the most part, and his ex-wife contends that he wasn't much better at home. She reports that he drinks straight out of the milk carton and puts the empty container back in the refrigerator. After buttering his toast, Bob leaves crumbs in the butter or adds jelly to his toast and dips back into the butter.

"The man obviously spent his junior high and high school lunch periods saying 'You gonna eat that?'" Debbie rants, "and he spent our entire marriage eating the last of whatever I was saving for later." Debbie went on to say that Bob almost never took a turn cooking, and if by some miracle he did, he'd leave all of the burnt, crusted pots and pans for her to clean. And what if Debbie refused to clean them? "Three days later he'd be complaining about all the dirty pots and pans stacked up in the sink!"

Although it seems impossible, Bob doesn't bother everyone. In fact, Edwin Phelps, Debbie's new husband, considers himself the benefactor of Big Bob's annoying habits. "Next to Bob," Edwin says while scratching his stomach and clearing his ear canal with a pencil, "I'm a regular Beau Brummell."

The entire staff of Bad Dog Press wishes you good luck, Debbie.

Another Annoying Worksheet

During your reading of this book you probably thought of a number of people in your life who possess some or all of the annoying traits listed herein. Before they slip blissfully from your mind, jot their names below. Then, help us all to rid the world of highly annoying people by purchasing them a gift copy of this book. They'll hopefully take the hint and mend their annoying ways.★

Annoying acquaintances who need this book:

_____

_____

_____

_____

_____

_____

★ *Again, we apologize for this annoying attempt to sell more of our books.*

Are You Annoying?

Take this little quiz:

1. At the video store, your first choice is a movie starring:

   a. Anthony Hopkins or Meryl Streep.

   b. Harrison Ford or Jodie Foster.

   c. Jerry Lewis.

2. In college you majored in:

   a. Biology or some other "hard science."

   b. Psychology or some other liberal art or "soft science" major.

   c. Acting.

3. After your significant other introduces you to his or her coworkers, they turn to him or her and say:

   a. "Where in the world have you been hiding this gem?"

   b. "It's about time we met ..."

   c. "You poor dear."

4. When someone mentions "classic American literature," you think of:

   a. *Moby Dick*

   b. *A Farewell to Arms*

   c. *The Bridges of Madison County*

5. Which of the following recent historic events gave you hope for the future:

   a. South Africa's abolishment of apartheid.

   b. The destruction of the Berlin Wall.

   c. The reunion of the Eagles.

6. You love pets. In fact, you own:

   a. A large dog.

   b. A medium-size dog.

   c. A yippy little dog, more than two cats, and/or any amount of reptiles.

7. You love your job …

   a. … publishing humor books.

   b. … performing potentially life-saving scientific research.

   c. … selling cars or insurance.

8. **You have successfully used the following phrase to help advance your career:**

   a. "I'll do it."

   b. "Great idea, boss."

   c. "You want fries with that?"

9. **Which statement best defines your fashion sense?**

   a. "Thank God for the timeless quality of blue jeans."

   b. "I'm not being 'trendy'—this is how I've always dressed."

   c. "The seventies are hip again? Groovy!"

10. **In your spare time, you:**

    a. Read enlightening books and magazines, listen to good music of various genres, or watch quality programming on television.

    b. Participate in some sport or community activity, perhaps even volunteer.

    c. Take those cheesy magazine and book quizzes.

How Did You Do?

Give yourself zero points for every time you answered "A", one point for every time you chose "B", and two points for each "C" response. Then just add them up and see where you fall on the chart below:*

   0 - 3   Normal.

   4 - 6   Somewhat Annoying.

   7 - 9   Annoying.

 10 - 12   Quite Annoying.

 13 - 15   Highly Annoying.

 16 - 18   Ultra Annoying.

 19 - 20   You received this book as an
                anonymous hint.

Before you proceed, check your response to Question 1. If you responded "C" (Jerry Lewis), there is no need to calculate the entire quiz. A "C" response indicates that you are French and, therefore, highly annoying by nature.

Before We Go …

You may have noticed that we spent a great deal of this book picking on the "art" of mime and the French. We think most of you will agree with our assessment of mime, but recognize that our seemingly relentless attack on the French could be construed as xenophobic (an annoyingly pretentious term meaning "hatred of anything strange or foreign"). We have no personal conflicts with the French, it's just that they're so annoyingly strange and foreign and, as a rule, make the best mimes. We would, however, be remiss if we did not point out the wonderful contribution France and its people have made to culture. After all, without the French there would be no Burger King® Croissanwich.™

OUR HIGHLY ANNOYING APPAREL SHOWS YOU HAVE:

A. A great sense of humor
B. Great taste in humor books
C. A limited wardrobe budget
D. A limited wardrobe
E. All of the above

TOILET SEAT UP *tee #HAP001*

> These make great gifts for that special annoying someone in your life.

LEAVES THE TOILET SEAT UP.

© BAD DOG, INC.

GET ME A BEER *tee #HAP002*

If you're close enough to read this, You're close enough to get me a beer.

© BAD DOG, INC.

ORDERING INFORMATION

You can order by mail* or phone.
Fill out this handy order form prior
to calling so you don't forget anything.

_____ Toilet Seat Up T-Shirt *(HAP001)* $17.95
_____ Get Me a Beer T-Shirt *(HAP002)* $17.95

_____ Bad Dog Logo T-Shirt *(BD001T)* $17.95
_____ Bad Dog Logo Sweat *(BD001S)* $27.95
_____ Bad Dog Embroidered Cap *(BD002)* $19.95
_____ Bad Dog Mug *(BD003)* $8.95
_____ Set of 4 Bad Dog Mugs *(BD004)* $25.00

XXL size t-shirts and sweats add $1.50
MN residents add 6.5% tax on non-apparel items
Allow two to three weeks for delivery
Shipping/handling charges: $5.00

Pick One:
☐ Free Button
☐ Free
   Bumper
   Sticker

◄ **FREE BUTTON**
OR BUMPER
STICKER
WITH
EVERY
ORDER

Sub Total Items $ _____
Tax $ _____
Shipping Charges $ ___$5.00___
Total $ _____

BAD DOG TOLL-FREE ORDER LINE
1-800-270-5863 VISA MasterCard

* To order by mail send your order with your name, address, phone
  with a check or money order to:
  Bad Dog Press P.O. Box 130066 Roseville, MN 55113

DO YOUR BAD DOG SHOPPING ON-LINE:
http://www.octane.com

BITE INTO THESE OTHER

BOOKS

They call when you're in the tub. They call during dinner. They call when you're "reading" in the bathroom. And whenever they call, they try to sell you something you more than likely don't want.

They're telemarketers, and Bad Dog Press's latest offering—*How to Get Rid of a Telemarketer*—presents dozens of hilarious ways to help readers regain precious spare time free of senseless solicitation and leave even the most tenacious telemarketers speechless.

Has your soul had enough chicken soup to make you gag? The souls at Bad Dog Press sure have, so to cleanse America's palate they're offering *Rubber Chickens for the Soul*, a parody of the popular, inspiration-laden *Chicken Soup for the Soul* books.

While the stories in Rubber Chickens may not exactly open the heart and rekindle the spirit like those in the "Chicken Soup" books, they'll at the very least rekindle your heartburn.

Perhaps you've never made the mistake of showing up for an interview wearing a tie that requires batteries or listing "donating plasma" under your résumé's employment experience section. Well, the authors of *Who Packed Your Parachute?* have, and they hope their book can help others to avoid making similar errors. Here is the complete guide to what NOT to do during a job search.

Who Packed Your Parachute is the perfect book for graduates, adult children living with their parents, and anyone else on a job search.

A WHOLE NEW BREED OF HUMOR BOOKS!

Like our namesakes, we at Bad Dog Press aren't afraid to dig in the trash, chew the furniture, or take off dragging the leash—but we do so with tasteful, funny books that will have you laughing all the way home from the bookstore.

As you read this, the folks at Bad Dog are busy preparing other books that you'll love! Watch your bookstore humor section for our latest releases.

HAVE A PEEK AT OUR FUTURE BOOKS!

Visit the BAD DOG Humor On-Line Web page to preview upcoming books, participate in fun contests, join in funny forums, and find out how you can contribute to future Bad Dog books.
http://www.octane.com